Let's Write Devotionals!

by

Melanie Stiles

Let's Write! Series – Book Two
Blue Jean Coach Publishing
Houston, Texas

Blue Jean Coach Publishing
109 N. Post Oak Lane, Ste. 525
Houston, Texas 77024

Access other books by Melanie at Amazon.com
or contact her at:
Melanie@MelanieStiles.com
www.MelanieStiles.com

ISBN -13: 978-1523472680
ISBN -10: 1523472685

Contents

"Stablish thy word unto thy servant,
who is *devoted* to thy fear."
Psalm 119:38 (KJV)

Introduction

Do you remember those simple, easy-to-understand, stories we read in kindergarten? I still recall the Dick, Jane and Spot adventures of my childhood. Perhaps you recall different stories. Did they open your world to the eventual dream of wanting to create your own manuscript? Perhaps you had additional experiences that ignited the fire within the writing portion of your soul. Either way, those tiny books definitely had the power to spark the beginning of a scribe yet to be born.

Experience has caused me to understand the tool most beneficial for the beginning writer is a primer; much like the small volumes we read when we attended school. *Let's Write! A No-Nonsense Manual* is Book One of a six-part series. *Let's Write Devotionals! A No-Nonsense Manual* is Book Two.

I've been writing devotionals for many years. I love the act of connecting the Word of God with my own reflections and personal experiences. I've been blessed to publish hundreds of them. My reader audiences for these short pieces have ranged from young girls and teens to adults. I believe every devotional has its own divine connection to another person or persons within God's kingdom.

If you have the desire to communicate through devotional writing, this little book will outline the process. Additionally, each chapter contains Decisive Devotional Exercises to help guide you on a practical level. I hope you'll take the time to work through them thoroughly. You'll notice scripture references at the end of each question. It helps to meditate on God's Word as you consider your responses.

I devoutly believe those with the passion to write must take on the effort of practicing their craft (write, write, write) as a lifelong endeavor. Each year can demonstrate how a writer's work drastically improves from one year to the next if he perseveres. As our minds are renewed through meditating on God's Word and seeking Him diligently, our words change in response. In this continual commitment is the message He intends to have passed onto the page.

It is my sincere prayer that you achieve your writing goals, while building your relationship with the One who gave you the desire to be a ready scribe in the first place.

You may want to take advantage of the book list on the RESOURCES page. The list will allow you to study further the content covered in *Let's Write Devotionals!*

The ABOUT THE AUTHOR page of this book details my contact information. Feel free to reach out and provide feedback on the series, ask questions, or simply let me know how your writing career is progressing. As a life coach and fellow author, I look forward to hearing from you!

Blessings and keep writing,

Melanie Stiles

1

D is for Devotionals

"True strength lies in submission
which permits one to dedicate his life,
through devotion, to something beyond himself. "
Henry Miller

I'm a firm believer in definitions, as in those listed in that old (probably beat up) dictionary I hope you have parked on your writing desk somewhere. And it's a good thing we own such trusty volumes, because we have to clear up something right here at the start of our devotional journey.

I've discovered there seems to be a bit of confusion, namely about two words – devotion and devotional. Do you know the difference? Perhaps we should begin here. If you don't happen to have your faithful writer's tool close, allow me to share from mine.

What Am I Writing Anyway?

Consider these definitions:

Devotion: love, loyalty, or enthusiasm for a person, activity or cause.

Devotional: of or used in religious worship.

If I've correctly interpreted, we write devotionals because we are devoted to God. With those writings, we are able to connect with other people who are also devoted to our Lord. What an exciting opportunity!

Having, I believe, accurately demonstrated the use of these words, you need to know not everyone will agree with me. In short, you will most certainly find the two words used interchangeably or even in opposite of my viewpoint. My intent here is to provide you with the terminology I have chosen for the purposes of this book. It is not to make a stand, correct or otherwise cause a point of debate with others (so, no emails please).

Let's Think Along These Lines

Writing devotionals similarly mirrors the work of a caricature artist. The goal of the craftsman is not to create a face exactly, but to produce a portrait that exaggerates the essence of a person. In order to begin, he must first spend hours learning to sketch human anatomy, especially facial structure. After all, noses, lips, cheeks and eyebrows, from person to person, have ample variety. Of course, he aims to become a master at drawing male and female figures of all ages, but that is not enough. He must also develop an eye that accurately translates what feature to exaggerate, while playing up prominent features and reducing the effect of non-prominent ones. Everything should be balanced in a way that achieves a reasonable likeness of the person he is drawing, yet highlighting a particular aspect of the individual.

I've "commissioned" several caricatures at various carnivals and fairs. Adorable scenarios of my likeness, riding a dolphin in my ten-gallon Texas cowgirl hat or holding hands with a buddy, have enriched my memories. Even the best of the best took no more than twenty minutes to complete. I wonder how many people consider the hours and hours of practice the artist has poured into those sleek strokes he artfully swipes on the page?

Devotionals contain the same deception. They look simple, yet are often ensconced in extensive labor that includes prayer, meditation and very careful writing. Devotional writers want to share with excellence what God has infused into their hearts because they want to help others deepen their relationship with Him.

Tools of the Trade

Just as the artist must gather his pencils, ink, paper and clipboard, a writer must gather supplies as well. Let's look at a few necessities.

Access to several translations of the Bible is crucial when entering the world of published devotionals. Work-for-hire publishers (which we will discuss in an ensuing chapter) can extend contract invitations for numerous devotionals, but, at the same time, they can also request a variety of Bible translations be used. Others may require one specific translation exclusively. Most devotional collections are geared toward sales to the general public with the awareness they are reading from many different Bible types.

A 2012 survey rated the top five translations in the United States as follows:

1. New International Version

2. King James Version

3. New Living Translation

4. New King James Version

5. English Standard Version.

In 2014, the King James moved up to first place. The list is perpetually shifting. It will most certainly change again in a year or two. There is no singular translation when it comes to writing devotionals.

Online resources are both free and often include an app for your smartphone or iPad. Here are five useful sites:

www.biblegateway.com

www.biblestudytools.com

www.bibleontheweb.com

www.blueletterbible.org

www.bible.org

A nice, fat **dictionary** is next on the list. Don't be tempted to use the online versions. They work well if you know exactly which word you want to check, but online sites leave no room for leafing through in inquisitive exploration. There are many opportunities to increase the quality of your words with a hard copy dictionary at hand.

A **synonym finder or thesaurus** is extremely helpful in avoiding repetition. Devotionals are composed of very few words and each needs to contribute fully to your completed body of work. Word repetition lessens the impact of your devotional message.

Bible concordances are indexes that relate directly to material in the Bible. A simple concordance lists Biblical words alphabetically, with numerical indications to enable the inquirer to find the appropriate passages where those words occur. They are particularly helpful when performing research on singular word studies or topics. When purchasing, be sure you note which Bible translation your concordance is meant to compliment.

Bible dictionaries provide definitions and additional information for the words found in the Bible. There are free online resources for these as well:

www.studylight.org/dictionaries

www.biblestudytools.com/dictionaries

Although it might be tempting to skip the acquisition of your devotional tools, you should consider the disservice you might be doing to yourself (and perhaps your service to God?) if you fail to prepare. In the publishing world, your reputation is, by necessity, based in one arena – the credibility represented by your words. A simple misquote or misinterpretation of scripture greatly affects how others (including both editors and audience) view your message.

Clarification, verification and meditation are the major tools we, as writers, employ to protect our own careers. Developing the patience to thoroughly vet every word, concept and scripture in every devotional falls under serving God in excellence.

Chapter One

Decisive Devotional Exercises

"I'm going to use all my tools, my God-given ability,
and make the best life I can with it."
LeBron James

1. What does it mean to you to be devoted to God?
    1 Samuel 12:24 (KJV)

2. How often do you seek God in prayer?
    1 Chronicles 16:11 (KJV)

3. What Bible study techniques do you currently have in place?
    2 Timothy 2:15 (KJV)

4. Where is your dedicated writing space? If you do not have a
    location, where could you establish one? Psalm 37:4 (KJV)

5. There are many options for collecting the tools of the trade –
    new, used, online resources or making use of your local
    library. What is your plan for collecting or using your tools
    when writing devotionals? Proverbs 3:5-6 (KJV)

2

Depth and Density

"To achieve some depth in your field requires a lot of sacrifices.
Want to or not, you're thinking about what you're doing in life
– in my case, dancing."
Mikhail Baryshnikov

An iceberg is commonly defined as a piece of ice that has calved or broken away from a glacier and become free-floating. Typically, around one-tenth of its mass can be seen above the surface of the water, with the bulk submerged under the ocean. We've seen the tip of the devotional iceberg in Chapter One. Now, let's explore what lies beneath.

A quality devotional has several carefully considered, behind-the-scenes aspects navigated by its writer. These include a preparation for battle with the enemy, creating an appropriate tone, and finding your own intimate place within yourself to access while writing. Your readers will actually see none of these components, yet they will miss them if a writer does less.

We Have an Opponent

As a Christian writer, we must know and accept, when we set out upon a spiritual path, we can expect to be met by a certain amount of spiritual resistance.

"For we wrestle not against flesh and blood, but against principalities, against powers, against the rulers of the darkness of this world, against spiritual wickedness in high places."
Ephesians 6:12 (NKJV)

Devotional writers can be quite surprised when they experience unexpected difficulties, emotional setbacks or general distractions as they attempt to write a message inclusive of God and His kingdom principles. What's a writer to do? The Bible gives us gives us a warning:

> "Be sober, be vigilant; because your adversary the devil, as a roaring lion, walketh about, seeking whom he may devour: Whom resist stedfast in the faith, knowing that the same afflictions are accomplished in your brethren that are in the world."
> 1 Peter 5:8-9 (KJV)

In paraphrase, you are not alone! As a believer, we all have to navigate battles with the same enemy.

Weapons for War

It's relatively easy to give this section of the book a fly-by-glance and think you don't need to review it. I encourage you not to ignore the very core of what has tripped up so many writers on their road to establishing a credible devotional writing and publishing experience. Writers who sidestep this particular issue often make remarks that sound seemingly unconnected, such as:

"I think I could write devotionals, but I never seem to find the time."

Or this one:

"Just when I was getting to the heart of my devotional, the phone continued to plague me non-stop."

And, finally, the declaration I honestly hate to hear:

"I've been meaning to get around to a devotional project for about two years now."

These statements may appear inconsequential, yet they have significant impact. May I ask you a soul-searching question? Are you brave enough to respond to it honestly? Here goes: **How long is God supposed to wait for you to get around to His work?**

The enemy has a long history of studying exactly what it takes to distract humans from the purposes of God. Fortunately, we have a long history to celebrate, too! We have a God who is mightier than the enemy. Let's look at a few suggestions for staying focused.

Recognize a continual renewing of our mind is necessary.
If we don't refresh our minds daily by reading God's Word and confessing we are who Christ says we are in Him, deterioration will slowly, but surely, occur. It manifests in lack of confidence, fear of risk, and a general acceptance of negative self-image concepts, particularly centered on our ability to write for Him. God gave us the

tools up front to battle these insecurities. We can always start with Romans 12:2, but we should add on additional scriptures until we have a confession worthy of addressing any and all of our weaknesses. Here is the first of many confessions:

"And be not conformed to this world: but be ye transformed by the renewing of your mind, that ye may prove what is that good, and acceptable, and perfect, will of God." Romans 12:2 (KJV)

Recognize we are all capable of opening the door to sin.

The enemy works diligently to lead people astray with what may appear to be desirable activities. Remember your writing pursuits constitute the perfect will of God. Your endeavors in this area should have value far above many other activities. It's up to us to sort out the priorities of our lifestyles in coordination with the Holy Spirit. The enemy's power is limited, while God's power is unlimited. Celebrate and give attention to your faith in Christ. Stand in your belief that you are in His will. Lastly, practice perpetually your ability to say "NO," especially if you are feeling pressure to move away from your calling. These spiritual disciplines help in retaining balance in our lives, as well as allowing us to make course corrections as needed. Proactivity is the key to avoiding the traps of the enemy, as this scripture details:

"Teaching us that, denying ungodliness and worldly lusts, we should live soberly, righteously, and godly, in this present world;"
Titus 2:12 (KJV)

Pray for increased wisdom and discernment. You're going to need it. The writing/publishing world is full of choices. That essentially means you'll be making a multitude of decisions as you consider what to write, where to submit your work and who you should network with along the way. God expects us to be proactive in the process. The Bible is full of action verbs: seek, knock, make, etc. In Ephesians 6:13 (KJV) and 1 Corinthians 16:13 (KJV) we are instructed to do ALL and *then stand* to wait for God's part in our journey.

We can be assured of receiving the knowledge we ask for, as promised by God. We can ask freely!

"If any of you lack wisdom, let him ask of God, that giveth to all men liberally, and upbraideth not; and it shall be given him."
James 1:5 (KJV)

Staying prepared for battle leaves our countenance in the appropriate condition to write what we desire – because it lines up with God's will.

Creating an Appropriate Tone

Consider how you feel when you participate in the following scenarios:

Weddings
Funerals
Birthday Parties
Christmas Church Services
Football Games
Your Prayer Closet

Human emotion ranges from sadness to joy. It can also run a gamut that includes: anger, distress, love, acceptance, shame, happiness, hope and more. When our feelings are aimed toward God, they can encompass worship, praise, anticipation and expectation. My small list – again – represents the tip of another iceberg, yet here lies the catalyst that will complete or destroy your devotional.

Emotions are the motivation behind action. They help us to survive and thrive. They are guides through life-changing decisions. Devotionals should be emotionally persuasive. When carefully considering your word usage, you create an opportunity for your reader to take a next step in the life God intends.

The depth of a devotional can be measured by its intended tone. Tones are defined by your choice of vocabulary. Certain pieces, such as those written for high holy days, should be postured reverentially. Others may take on the job of encouragement, inspiration or motivation to overcome specific obstacles.

A quality devotional starts from a place rooted in your own personal relationship with God. While a writer's voice is both consistent and sincere, tones shift accordingly from devotional to devotional.

Spending Time in the Secret Place

I'm no pastor, preacher or theologian; nevertheless, there is a requirement of devotional writing that must be addressed in this vein. Let's take a look at the biblical passage below:

"But thou, when thou prayest, enter into thy closet, and when thou hast shut thy door, pray to thy Father which is in secret; and thy Father which seeth in secret shall reward thee openly."
Matthew 6:6 (KJV)

In context, this scripture speaks to the value of private prayer vs. prayers seen by others as religious acts in relation to receiving reward (see verses surrounding Matthew 6:6). But some have taken this warning by Jesus a step further and established what is commonly called a "prayer closet." A prayer closet is as unique as its owner. Comfortable chairs, tables, Bibles and note-taking paraphernalia can be placed in a specified room, a quiet corner or in patio spaces. I've met people who created their prayer closet in an actual closet. Others use the same bench in the park or the same table at the local coffee shop every morning.

There are valid reasons for having a dedicated prayer location. Perhaps this goes beyond what Jesus was referring to in the scripture, but it is a great way to declare boundaries and routines. It's important for a devotional writer to do what he/she must to consistently foster an intimate relationship with God. By necessity, interruptions should not be tolerated. God seeking requires a certain amount of solitude. We must step away from the hustle and bustle of human life.

God is in this secret place. It is here we discover clarity in His purposes for our lives, as well as for our work. It is where we receive encouragement, solutions and refreshment. If you have not declared a daily space and routine, your devotionals will lack the depth and density needed to impact others. They will only skim the

tip of your devotional iceberg.

Chapter Two

Decisive Devotional Exercises

"I avoid looking forward or backward,
and try to keep looking upward."
Charlotte Bronte

1. Do you acknowledge we, as Christians, have a common enemy? If so, define how he has affected you in various instances. If not, why not?
Ephesians 6:11-18 (KJV)

2. Describe your disciplines concerning the renewing of your mind. Philippians 4:8 (KJV)

3. List the action verbs in the following scripture passages: Matthew 7:7 (KJV), Matthew 28:19 (KJV) and Ezra 10:4 (KJV).

4. Revisit the list of scenarios listed in this chapter. Record a few of your emotional experiences from any of the events. Ecclesiastes 3:1 (KJV)

5. Do you have a prayer closet? If so, describe why it works for you. If not, where could you create one? What would you place in your space? Jeremiah 33:3 (KJV)

3

Distinctive Details

"It's the little details that are vital.
Little things make big things happen."
John Wooden

Tight writing and the handling of scripture are two aspects of writing that can be viewed as directly relating to all written material, however, they carry particular weight for devotionals. Both topics have the power to show your work deemed ready for publication or relegated to the slush (rejection) pile by an editor.

What is Tight Writing?

When completing my certifications as a Christian Life Coach, I noticed the course contained an inordinate amount of material on one particular subject – listening. After several years of client interaction, I understand why the training was so intensive. Some people are very skilled at getting to the point in conversation, while others start with the year they were born and move forward from there – no matter the topic. It's time to be honest again. If you're a birth-to-today writer, devotionals are going to be a lesson in brevity. Why? Devotionals have word count ranges from 100 to 700, with 250 words being about average. Picture a single, double-spaced, typewritten page. You have very few lines to convey a complete message. Every word has tremendous value. There is no room for wandering away to explore a sub-topic in a devotional. No space for redundancy. Each sentence must contribute to the bigger picture being painted.

Tight Write Tips

1. **Practice, practice and more practice.** This old adage will never go away. The more we write, the better we write. By giving yourself a topic and a word count, you learn how to express your ideas within a specific parameter.

2. **Know your beginning, middle and end BEFORE you start writing.** There is no winding and weaving your way through a devotional, anymore than there is a winding or weaving in most jobs. Yes, we are creative vessels, but by the time we sit down to produce, the devotional has moved to a crafting action. It's time to take off your designer/creativity hat and replace it with a more practical one.

3. **Scrutinize every single word choice.** Think about your dresser drawers. They will only hold so much. If you continue to purchase items that need to be stored there, something will have to go or you'll have a mangled mess. It's logical to presume the least appealing apparel would be discarded. The goal for a devotional is to have only the very

best material included. We, as writers, must actively choose which word is better than another for our specific topic.

4. **Detach yourself emotionally from the project.** We tend to fall in love with our own work. Keep in mind, the piece is not meant for you. It's a gift given to others, through you, but from the Lord. To write within this spiritual commitment, we must retain our spiritual objectivity.

5. **Read your piece out loud.** It's vital to ascertain where words don't flow. If your tongue trips up on a sentence, phrase or word, it's likely that your reader's concentration will do the same. It is also wise to have three "sample readers." You'll want to pick these three carefully. Consider your readers in view of the following: their ability to give honest feedback on content, knowledge of grammar/punctuation and willingness to support your efforts in general. You never want a reader who tells you everything is always wonderful. You also do not want one who exclusively criticizes your work.

Pesky Passivity

To write or not to write passively - even Shakespeare had to consider the question. Yet, many writers fail to give the topic the attention it deserves - especially when having such a tiny devotional space. Passive verbs and voice are valid grammar/style tools; but in the end, we are the wordsmiths who must decide what works best for a devotional. Let's look at this simple example:

Active Voice Example

The author wrote the devotional.

Passive Voice Example

A devotional has been written by the author.

Which sentence seems more direct to you? Which seems concise and clear? Passive applications often confuse or blur a subject; consequently, a writer loses connection with the reader. Never forget devotionals are centered on connection. It is their very purpose.

An easy way to eradicate the majority of passive statements in your work is to chase constructions in the form of "to be," such as: is, are, am, was, were, has been, have been, had been, will be, will have been, and being. Isolate and study these sentences. Attempt to rewrite them using the example above. Aim to remove nouns followed by verb phrases. Instead, try a noun, verb, and noun *again* setup example. The process of removing passivity will automatically result in a clearer message for your reader. For a further refresher course, please see books listed on the Resources page of this book.

Beyond the 100

How many of the most popular Bible verses in the Christian world could you quote? Do you even know what those prevalent verses are? It might interest you to know you'll have to expend minimal energy to find out. A simple Google search will net you at least a dozen lists. They don't vary much. But why should you care? These are the verses that will naturally pop into your head when attempting to write a devotional. It's important to remember there are approximately 31,000 more verses from which to choose. I'm not trying to lecture anyone about appreciating the Bible in its entirety. I'm asking you to avoid what appears to be currently trending scripture if possible. Of course, there exists a core mainstay of relevant passages. I'm encouraging you to take the time to read and study further.

There are two types of devotionals you're likely to write. The first comes only from you - creating your piece and adding a scripture passage you have personally selected. The other type is an assigned devotional. Assignments come from publishing houses with which you've signed a contract and agreed to write for hire (to be discussed later). The editor will assign specific passages and you will be expected to write your devotionals with those in mind.

There are other reasons for going beyond the 100 easily sought verses. Studying Old Testament stories and less popular scripture passages creates opportunities to establish unique relationships between our lifestyles today vs. those of the ancients. In looking back, we are connecting to our Christian roots and values. These unions can be expressed in devotional form.

We have no real way of knowing how many people in our culture are depending on devotional reading to learn the precepts of Christianity. I suspect this number is higher than we might want to admit, given there are statistics that say a mere 7% of all Christians read the Bible daily. Let's try an experiment. Ask twenty people, in your own community, if they read the Word of God daily. More than half of my focus group responded with, "Oh yes! I read a daily devotional every morning."

A devotional can be the tool that inspires, motivates or urges a reader to delve into the Bible of his own volition.

The Preacher in You

Everyone has a moral code. Let's call it a conscience. Not all moral codes match because, as humans, we've been submerged in opinion, denial, shame, sin, etc.... Christians have the added inclusion of the Holy Spirit, working in tandem with conscience or code. Our codes, given personality traits, personal experiences and other factors can unite with a subject of interest to conjure a cause. What does this mean for the devotional writer?

Let's say you have a write-for-hire assignment that includes the following scripture:

"For the woman which hath an husband is bound by the law to her husband so long as he liveth; but if the husband be dead, she is loosed from the law of her husband."
Romans 7:2 (KJV)

Seeing this scripture thrills you, because you have never believed in divorce. You have been married to the same man – for better or for worse – for twenty years. This is your moment to let the world know divorce is not an option! Or is it your moment? If your job, as a devotional writer, is to connect with your reader, how will

43

your words resonate with a newly divorced woman who is desperately seeking God for clarity and peace in her life? How will telling her divorce is bad prevent her from feeling awful – even when it was her husband who filed, because he's "no longer in love" with her?

New cause-filled writers can have tremendous urges to outright preach a viewpoint within a body of work. In doing so, they become an audience of one. Devotionals are meant to focus on God, not human opinion. They are designed to let the unloved know God loves them. Always, always, always, we should be asking ourselves why our opinions even matter, as they stand up against an all-forgiving God. There are far better messages to write than preachy, opinionated works. Every message can be couched in Christ. In the end, if we allow God to be God and understand we are to be a vessel of His instruction, our work will bear His truths.

Chapter Three

Decisive Devotional Exercises

"I used to think the worst thing in life
was to end up all alone, it's not.
The worst thing in life is to end up with people
that make you feel all alone."
Robin Williams

1. Are you a birth-to-today writer? If so, how can you prevent adding unneeded details to your devotionals?
    Luke 10:42 (KJV)

2. Practice tight writing by picking any verse in this chapter and writing a devotional body of 250 words. Psalm 77:12 (KJV)

3. Show your practice devotional to three readers to receive feedback. Matthew 5:16 (KJV)

4. Google and study one of the Top 100 Scripture lists. Romans 15:4 (KJV)

5. Instead of writing about your cause, how can you physically do something to support your beliefs? Titus 3:9 (KJV)

4

Delivering Your Message

"Reputation is what men and women think of us;
character is what God and angels know of us."
Thomas Paine

Imagine you have been invited to attend a State Dinner at the White House. No need to hesitate. This is definitely a bucket list, once-in-a-lifetime experience. You decide to splurge on the finery, douse yourself in expensive perfume and arrange your countenance to be on your absolute best behavior.

The evening begins without disappointment. You are appropriately dazzled with the night's festivities and, before long, are escorted regally into the State Dining Room for your five-course meal. As you are seated, you discreetly notice the place card nestled next to yours is that of, none other than, the King of Abracadabra. You are dining in the presence of kings!

Eventually, the King eases into his chair alongside you. He turns to introduce himself, lifting your hand and gently placing a kiss on your knuckle. Oh my!

As the crab soup is served, you deftly drape your napkin over your lap. Yet, you can't help but notice; the King doesn't make the same effort. In fact, he hurriedly snatches up the spoon meant for dessert and slurps his way through a bowl of excellently prepared food!

Weeks later, your friends are still asking you to describe your adventure. The King is always a part of the tale – but for all the wrong reasons. Your story perpetually ends on the same note.

"I would definitely do it again, but <u>not</u> with the King as a meal companion."

Interestingly, one exhibition of poor etiquette has become the essence of the man.

As writers, we create our own essence with every word. When approaching how the craft of writing relates to devotionals, it is just as important to cover the "don'ts" as it is to explore the "do's." Avoiding certain devotional blunders can open many more publishing doors and further our goals of reaching an intended audience.

DO

Make sure the piece you write focuses on God. Writing devotionals for any other reason than to communicate some aspect of God – His love, mercy, grace, etc. – is equivalent to a useless gesture. It defeats the very definition of devotionals.

DON'T

Make "you" the primary figure in your work. Use the word "I" sparingly. Strive to show or paint a picture, rather than tell your story. Make use of story elements such as sensory details, descriptions and conversation.

DO

Depend on being Spirit led – no matter how long it takes. In our drive-through-to-get-everything American culture, it would seem quite natural to assume you do not need to wait upon the Lord, yet that is not how God works. Devotional writers commit themselves to the process of turning away from distraction, carving out blocks of time devoted to seeking solitude and meditation. They are aware of having spiritual ears and wait expectantly, ready to listen. His answer has and will always come in His timing.

DON'T

Write off the top of your head, failing to dig deeper. Every writer faces deadline dilemma. The key is NOT to push words on a page at the last minute. Instead, prepare by providing yourself the time to process and pray.

DO

Keep a scripture/mediation journal. Many devotionals write themselves, while you are exploring your own God experience within a journal. Additionally, we all have scripture passages that we hold dear. A journal is the best place to organize your thoughts and impressions around them. You may not use everything in your journal, but you will extend your knowledge of the Word of God, which, in turn, contributes to your writing in the future.

DON'T

Fail to learn from your writing experiences. All growth happens over time. It can be quite beneficial to go back and review journal entries. Measuring our own spiritual growth gives us insight into the processes of our audience. We constantly stand in the middle of the road. There will always be those who are more mature and those who are less. Both groups make up the devotional writer's audience.

DO

Establish your takeaway from the beginning. A takeaway is essential to every devotional. A variety of takeaways exist, but essentially provide a reader with something he can walk away thinking about or doing.

Takeaways induce your reader to:

- Learn something new and interesting

- Laugh or experience some type of joy

- Feel better understood

- Accomplish a task or project – either physically, spiritually or emotionally

- Be motivated toward a physical action.

If written correctly, every devotional contains such a takeaway.

DON'T

Attempt multiple lessons/themes in one devotional. It's possible for a writer to believe she has written one devotional, when in fact, she has written the beginning for two or more. Make use of the three sample readers you've selected, as their insight is invaluable. Good devotional writing is exploratory, but only with one topic per piece.

DO

Pray over your assigned scripture. The terminology in 1 Corinthians 3:9, written by Paul, the apostle, makes clear to us that we are "God's fellow workers." The passage goes on to state others have laid foundations before us and it is our responsibility to build upon what is already good and serves the purposes of God. By praying over the scripture we are assigned, we open ourselves to the message God would have us to convey in due season. It is something to be taken seriously as it relates directly to the Christian body He has amassed on our planet.

DON'T

Hesitate to change the direction of your writing, as you are Spirit led. Devotional writing considers and asks questions. It is open to both God revelation and self-revelation. It encompasses the evaluation of scripture and how it applies to daily life experiences. If a writer is urged by Holy Spirit inspiration/instruction to drop a direction and proceed in another, he/she is blessed with connection.

DO

Envision and pray for your audience. In the book of Exodus, Moses prayed for his audience. He believed his communication with God would pave the way for the message he was to deliver. If we do not consider our audience when writing devotionals, how can we be assured of its receipt? Your prayers will align your message with its intent, as surely as an arrow flies toward the center of a champion archer's target.

Summing It Up

Every devotional writer must establish a method for connecting experiences (either personal, Biblical or someone else's) with a scriptural teaching that causes a reader to reflect on his own life. In developing a piece, the writer must decide how vulnerable and open he will be about the lessons he's learned. By weaving story, a heart connection is created through empathy, identification and sympathy. Authenticity paves the way to sharing personal faith and growth. Growth is not about knowing all the answers, merely suggesting we think about what matters to God and His disciples.

Chapter Four

Decisive Devotional Exercises

"Learn to get in touch with the silence within yourself,
and know that everything in life has purpose.
There are no mistakes, no coincidences,
all events are blessings given to us to learn from."
Elisabeth Kubler-Ross

1. How important is it to you to primarily focus on God when writing and why? Matthew 6:33 (KJV)

2. How accustomed are you to waiting to be led by the Holy Spirit? Psalm 27:14 (KJV)

3. Do you believe God is able to speak through your devotional? Hebrews 1:1 (KJV)

4. Are you willing to study and perform the necessary research prior to writing a devotional? Proverbs 16:3 (KJV)

5. Can you envision your audience? Describe them. Galatians 3:28-29 (KJV)

5

Design Matters

"Design is so simple. That's why it's so complicated."
Paul Rand

My grandmother plied her seamstress skills to the task of creating tablecloths for all the recognized holidays in our household. Consequently, I have the ability to decorate for literally every occasion. It's easy to pull out what I need from my stack of twelve. I just look at the design on the fabric. Not so with devotional design. While certain core elements exist, multiple variables come into play. This can be confusing to the writer who believes all devotionals are decorated in the same way.

Core Components...Generally Speaking

A trip to the nearest bookstore, along with a short perusal of the spiritual inspiration aisle, will produce the necessary research needed to understand there is a general consistency in the format of devotionals. At a quick glance, they will all look similar because certain sections are almost always included. A writer who chooses to self publish, freelance or write work-for-hire will need to be familiar with the elemental basics.

Devotionals generally have a time frame designation. The overall period a manuscript covers may vary. Most are orchestrated for daily reading; hence each devotional will have an actual date or day designation. These books are designed in various durations.

Typical titles announce 30-day, 90-day and one-year formats. This is not a hard and fast rule. Some bodies of work combine other aspects of devotional writing, such as Bible study questions or reflection questions that allow a longer period in between readings (52 week devotionals; one per week for a year).

Devotionals generally are titled. Just as the devotional piece is short, the title should follow suit. Consider the headlines on the front page of any newspaper. They are devised to get your attention. A title's purpose and intention is to cause the reader to further engage with the content or body of the article.

Devotionals generally point to a key scriptural verse. This does not mean only one verse will be recommended. There are formats that list a multi-verse passage, while only highlighting one verse to be referenced within the reading. Double and triple checking verses and translations is good practice for every devotional writer. A writer's credibility is greatly bruised if errors occur in this particular part of his/her submission.

Devotionals have a message generally referred to as a body, anecdote, meditation or reflection. The language may change from publication to publication. A good practice is to read through submission guidelines carefully until the terms and definitions become clear.

Devotionals have a closing section, generally referred to as a prayer or a call to action. It's common to have both a prayer and a call to action within the closing section of a devotional. Prayers are often given very small word counts as the publication reserves as many words as possible for the main body of the piece. The prayer is a direct response to the message written by its author.

What Can Change...

Translation preferences change depending on the publication. This aspect of devotional writing is non-negotiable. In certain instances, a verse, familiar to a writer in one translation, can take on new context in another. A writer never assumes a different translation will be close enough. Scripture quotes must be written exactly. In that preciseness, maximum impact is created between devotional body and verse. Copyright laws exist for all Bible translations (except the King James Version). Instructions which outline the number of verses an author may use without acquiring a permission request can be found on the website of the Bible's publisher.

Overall word count can change depending on the publication. Some publications tally a word count that includes scripture, body, and prayer. Others may gauge word count only using body and prayer, and exclude scripture. Still others use only the body. Guidelines are a writer's best friend when moving from one publication to another.

Vocabulary can change depending on the age range of an audience. When writing to adults, the subject matter and vocabulary rarely exceeds a 12th grade reading level. Beyond this age bracket, there are many opportunities to write devotionals for children, teens and young adults. Take the time to find out what challenges these age groups view as significant. Learn their language levels. It's helpful to conduct interviews or chats with a few members of your focus audience to get a sense of the age range culture and trending jargon.

Byline locations can change depending on the publication. Bylines may be placed, as is standard, directly on a writer's work. They may also be found in the back of a book, all contributors listed alphabetically with a short author's bio (biography). In some cases, particularly when writing work-for-hire, there may not be a byline opportunity at all. Preparing a 50-word author bio in advance that expresses some aspect of an author's life is advisable. Check out other author bios as examples.

Pronoun preferences can change depending on the publication. Occasionally, an editor will request the avoidance of masculine pronouns – either in reference to God or in reference to people in general. This doesn't change the nature of a message if it is written well.

Additional items can be added. Depending on the book format, other items can be included with a devotional such as quotes, hymn references, or specific terminology that is part of a theme. If an editor expects a writer to provide such information, it will be in the guidelines. The publisher may prefer to insert supplemental details themselves.

Chapter Five

Decisive Devotional Exercises

"Design is not just what it looks like and feels like.
Design is how it works."
Steve Jobs

1. Practice creating three titles for the devotional body you wrote for the Chapter Three Decisive Exercises No. 2. Genesis 2:20a (KJV)

2. Consider your prayer style. Do you pray long, flowing prayers? Short concise prayers? Write out a prayer for your devotional, using 50 words or less. Luke 17:5 (KJV)

3. How many Bible translations are you familiar with? Are you comfortable using various translations? If not, why not? 2 Timothy 3:16 (KJV)

4. How do you feel about writing for audiences younger than yourself? 1 Thessalonians 2:8 (KJV)

5. Are you comfortable working without a byline? Under what conditions would you consider doing so? John 5:30 (KJV)

6

Divine Destinations

"Follow what you are genuinely passionate about and
let that guide you to your destination."
Diane Sawyer

We are down to the final chapter in our devotional writing journey. I have some news that may – or may not – come as a shock. Ready? Writing devotionals for publication will not make you rich. I view this niche as falling directly under the category of a calling. Inside every calling there is a measure of labor unto the Lord. Publishing devotionals is no exception. After a devotional is written and perfected, there is still the job of submitting the work. If we fail to follow through, we block our messages from reaching their divine destinations.

There Are Several Ways to Publish

Blogs, Facebook and other nonpaying avenues are instantly available. Many writers post devotionals on social media outlets. Others are "employed" by groups and churches to write. These are valuable opportunities to adjust to deadlines, formats and topic requests. It's also not uncommon for a writer to tithe her time and gifts, while continuing to publish for pay in other arenas. There is a caveat that can interfere with a writer if he/she is unaware. Nothing you publicly publish in these nonpaying markets should be used for submission to a paying market. You will need new material.

Editors frown on previously published submissions, as a rule. If in doubt, consult the writer's guidelines for the publication.

Creating devotional books through self-publishing venues gives a writer total control of the product. Unfortunately, in the excitement of being able to publish a book absolutely free of charge through CreateSpace/Kindle, a writer can fail to see what else she is responsible for to complete the publishing process. Consequently, many books are poorly uploaded and even more poorly edited. The writer's reputation suffers accordingly. Also, book sales rest on the shoulders of how big the writer's existing audience is and how she is promoting the book. There are tons of books resting idly on Amazon with no orders placed. An action plan should be created to market the book and the author.

Freelancing individual devotionals provides a writer with a history of publishing credits and, sometimes, payment. Creating a reputation as an established, published devotional writer can lead to further assignments. Relationships with editors are priceless, so they must be protected by responsible and timely submissions. There are many, many markets to choose from. It is wise to study both the guidelines and an actual issue of any publication before submitting.

Every publication has its own culture and vocabulary. Markets can be found through online searches and through Writers Market books (see the Resources page). Opportunities encompass submissions to newsletters, websites, Sunday school papers, magazines, blogs and more. Take note of the distribution of the market. Some publications have a reach of many thousand readers. Be aware of denominational parameters. Faith and belief interpretations vary.

Assignment work means more devotionals to write. Many publishers issue annual devotional books. These editors are looking for writers who can write batches of devotionals to a specific guideline. Traditionally, an editor will request that a writer submit a number of sample devotionals as an "audition" for placement within a group they continually offer assignments. This group of writers is often referred to as a stable. If accepted into the stable, it is not unusual to receive assignment contract offers regularly.

Work-for-hire is harder to get, but the quantity and pay are greater. Larger publishing houses package gift books in devotional (and other formats, such as prayer books or promise books) form. For a 365-day devotional, they may employ as many as 30-40 writers, each signing a contract to write a 10-12 devotional portion. The best way to access work-for-hire editors is to study the Writers Market and network with other work-for-hire writers.

Pitching a gift book to a large publishing house is possible. Many writers' conferences invite acquisition editors to be available for "pitches." These professionals know what type of book has a chance at success with the company's purchase committee. A pitch is a short television-commercial-type presentation outlining the premise of a book. It can be given orally or written. If the pitch falls into an area the house specializes in, the editor will ask for a book proposal. Devotionals are considered nonfiction. You can find both nonfiction and fiction book proposal templates online. Please note there is a difference between the two. A book proposal is a work of art within itself. At approximately 20-30 pages, it explores many aspects about a book's potential including premise, salability, competition, format and more. Prior to attending any conference, a writer should research the houses represented by the acquisition editors available. Each has distinct areas of promotion. Never pitch to a house that does not publish devotionals. If a house publishes devotionals, research the format they are accustomed to selling.

The Optimum Tool for Submitting Your Work

It's time for me to share my key verse as it relates to writing and publishing devotionals:

> "And God is able to make all grace abound toward you;
> that ye, always having all sufficiency in all things,
> may abound to every good work:"
> 2 Corinthians 9:8 (KJV)

The most useful tool any writer can store up is the confidence to push forward, no matter how he feels. It's natural to experience timidity or insecurity when facing new adventures. Risk is part of the journey. As writers, we tend to be far more comfortable expressing our hearts through our work. But that is only half of the process. We must stand in faith that we are called to write for others.

Invite people to come closer to God through your words. Relate your personal experiences, so others who are struggling will know they are not alone. Lead your readers into further intimacy and honesty. You don't need to have all the answers. Your mission is to aid your reader in taking the next step of faith in God. Encourage and create a safe place to embrace the One Who made us all.

Chapter Six

Decisive Devotional Exercises

"By prevailing over all obstacles and distractions, one may
unfailingly arrive at his chosen goal or destination."
Christopher Columbus

1. How important do you think receiving payment for your
   devotionals is to God? Matthew 19:30 (KJV)

2. Can you think of any possible volunteer writing opportunities
   in your community? List them with contact information.
   1 Timothy 5:17 (KJV)

3. Can you envision writing an entire devotional book? Create
   your development plan for the book. How many devotionals?
   What is your overall theme? Philippians 4:13 (KJV)

4. How willing are you to risk when it comes to submitting your
   work? Psalm 27:1 (KJV)

5. Do you believe you were meant to connect people and God
   through your words? How do you intend to do that?
   Luke 8:39 (KJV)

RESOURCES

Eats, Shoots & Leaves: The Zero Tolerance Approach to Punctuation
by Lynne Truss
ISBN-10: 1502402038

The Synonym Finder by J.I. Rodale
ISBN-10: 0446370290

The Christian Writer's Market Guide 2015-2016: Everything You Need to Get Published
by Jerry B. Jenkins
ISBN-10: 1404103058

Writer's Market 2016: The Most Trusted Guide to Getting Published 95th Edition
by Robert Lee Brewer
ISBN-10: 1599639378

The Heart of a Ready Scribe: 52 Reflections for Writers
by Melanie Stiles
ISBN-10: 1462014399

Let's Write! A No-Nonsense Manual
by Melanie Stiles
ISBN-10: 1493570307

SAMPLE DEVOTIONAL

Excerpt from: *The Heart of a Ready Scribe:*
52 Reflections for Writers
by Melanie Stiles

THE NEED TO BE HEARD

Week 2
"Why do writers write? Because it isn't there."
Thomas Berger

Do the names Edison, Bell, Whitney and Davy mean anything to you? Okay, I'll admit I cheated with Davy. Thomas Alva Edison invented the phonograph, but only improved the electric light. Davy was fifty years ahead of him with the discovery.

These are all men of legacy. Men who knew something was possible, even if at first, they hadn't yet found a way to prove it. And because they doggedly remained true to an idea, you and I now reap immense benefit.

Consider for a moment what our lives would be like if even one of them had given up too soon. Surely, you say, someone else would have come along and done the same thing. That may be true. Nevertheless, you also cannot deny that the history of the light bulb, the explosion of manufacturing, and even the model of your own cell phone might not yet be as advanced as they are today.

These men, like us, stood inside their passion until it came to fruition. Close your eyes. Can you see your finished manuscript in your hand? How about that cover art?

The Master Author Says...
  For we walk by faith not by sight.
  2 Corinthians 5:7 (KJV)

Reflections
What single message is in your heart right now? Who could benefit from that internal song your scribe heart plays repeatedly? Use this week to explore and pray for those who are waiting to read your words. Make a list of who they are.

SCRIPTURE REFERENCES
NOTE: ONLY KING JAMES TRANSLATIONS HAVE BEEN CITED IN THIS BOOK.

OLD TESTAMENT

Genesis 2:20a
1 Samuel 12:24
1 Chronicles 16:11
Ezra 10:4
Psalm 27:1
Psalm 27:14
Psalm 37:4
Psalm 77:12
Psalm 119:38
Proverbs 3:5-6
Proverbs 16:3
Ecclesiastes 3:1
Jeremiah 33:3

NEW TESTAMENT

Matthew 5:16
Matthew 6:6
Matthew 6:33
Matthew 7:7
Matthew 19:30
Matthew 28:19
Luke 8:39
Luke 10:42
Luke 17:5
John 5:30
Romans 7:2
Romans 12:2
Romans 15:4
1 Corinthians 3:9
1 Corinthians 16:13
2 Corinthians 9:8
Galatians 3:28-29

NEW TESTAMENT -CONTINUED

Ephesians 6:11-18
Ephesians 6:12
Ephesians 6:13
Philippians 4:8
Philippians 4:13
1 Thessalonians 2:8
2 Timothy 2:15
2 Timothy 3:16
2 Timothy 5:17
Titus 2:12
Titus 3:9
Hebrews 1:1
James 1:5
1 Peter 5: 8-9

ABOUT THE AUTHOR

Melanie Stiles is a Christian Life Coach and author blessed with a rich freelance writing history. She has enjoyed hundreds of bylines in genres ranging from journalistic reporting to award-winning poetry. Her book, *The Heart of a Ready Scribe: 52 Reflections for Writers*, has been awarded honors in both the 2012 Indie Excellence Awards and the 2014 Xulon Christian Choice Book Awards. As a frequent speaker at writer's conferences and women's venues, Melanie uses her background to instruct, inspire and celebrate life journeys with others. As a Christian Life Coach, Melanie is invested in helping writers, but also all individuals who want to achieve the desires of the heart.

Melanie is currently working on a six-part mini-book series for new writers intent on pursuing a freelance career.

Book One, Let's *Write! A No-Nonsense Manual*, provides writers with the very basic, bare-bones components needed to accomplish goals of writing and publishing.

Book Two, *Let's Write Devotionals! A No-Nonsense Manual*, takes writers through the in's and out's of devotional writing and submitting to this special market.

Melanie would love to hear about your writing pursuits or life challenges.
Email her at Melanie@MelanieStiles.com

83

www.ingramcontent.com/pod-product-compliance
Lightning Source LLC
Chambersburg PA
CBHW062058280526
45788CB00003B/1272